The Return of the Musical Prophet

Understanding the transforming power of music and sound

STEVE ABLEY

RIVER
PUBLISHING

River Publishing & Media Ltd
Barham Court
Teston
Maidstone
Kent
ME18 5BZ
United Kingdom

info@river-publishing.co.uk

ISBN 978-1-908393-44-9
Printed in the United Kingdom

Contents

Dedication

This book is dedicated to the two most amazing and beautiful people in my life.

Trace, you are the most incredible wife. I have never met anyone with the capacity to love like you do. You have so much insight into so many people's lives and situations, yet you remain calm, patient, kind, witty and non-judgemental with everyone, including me. You epitomize everything expressed at the end of Proverbs and I will love you always.

"Many women do noble things, but you surpass them all." (Proverbs 31:29)

Harriet, you astound me with everything you are and do in life. I could never have wished for a better daughter in any respect. The compassion and mercy you show is stunning; the strength and tenacity you have to go the extra mile whenever and wherever it is needed is priceless; and then there's that sense of humour! The dreams you have are huge and totally achievable with the resources you have at your disposal. I am immensely proud of you and will always love you.

"'For I know the plans I have for you,' declares the Lord, 'plans to prosper you and not to harm you, plans to give you a hope and a future.'" (Jeremiah 29:11)

Acknowledgements

I am so grateful to all those who have taken an interest in this project – for lending me their expertise, offering advice and checking the principles contained within. Thank you especially to:

Jonathan Bugden

Rowena Burrows

Ian Hardman

Miriam Hearn

Myrtle Lawrence

I am particularly indebted and thankful to Peter Davey for the long hours of proof reading, grammar correction and generous encouragement.

Thank you all so much.

Foreword

The first time the word "band" is ever mentioned or defined in history is in the story of 1 Samuel 10. This is not a reference to a group of performing musicians, come together to entertain an audience at a concert. Rather, it establishes a precedent for how bands are designed for function according to God's word.

In this outlandish, never-seen-before story, we find a procession of prophets coming down from a high place. Samuel tells Saul that as he approaches a certain town,

"...you will meet a band of prophets coming down from the place of worship. They will be playing a harp, a tambourine, a flute, and a lyre, and they will be prophesying." (1 Samuel 10:5 NLT)

We see a band of prophets who are not only walking boldly across enemy territory (the Philistine's high place) whilst playing their instruments, but they are prophesying as well! Even crazier than this, we notice that Saul did not seem very alarmed by the situation. He treated it like it was an everyday occurrence in this season of history.

Saul followed the prophet's advice and was anointed on that day, taking up the mantle of king. But that anointing only came upon him in the company of these prophesying minstrels.

"The Spirit of the LORD will come powerfully upon you, and you will prophesy with them; and you will be changed into a different person. Once these signs are fulfilled, do whatever your hand finds to do, for God is with you." (v6-7)

In Burn 24-7 we have taken this biblical precedent seriously and have commissioned similar "bands" of musicians all over the world. During the last seven years many furnaces of prophetic worship have been ignited – and in similarly unlikely places: the red light district of Amsterdam; the warzones of Iraq, North Korea and Congo; the urban sprawls of Japan and India; amongst the unreached portions of the Himalayas and in over 50 nations, among countless people groups!

From the high places to the low places, we are bent on seeing the presence of God invade the nations. We are only just beginning to witness the start of the harvest of transformation that is the "knowledge of the Lord … filling the whole earth" (Habakkuk 2:2).

This is not a NEW thing in history or some genius concept that man has come up with. It is an old truth that God is reawakening and reviving in his Church in this hour. It is simply a "returning to the ancient paths."

Allow the pages of this book, its testimonies, stories and Scripture lead you into this incredible global adventure. The musical prophets are rising again!

Sean Feucht
Global Founder of The Burn 24-7

Introduction

One day in the summer of 2009, I was sitting in a café at Camden Lock Market when I had the most profound and life changing experience. For those unfamiliar with Camden, it is a really exciting place, just north of central London and quite unlike any other area of the city. The market is a vibrant blend of cultures, peoples and beliefs, with just about every social group and world culture represented. The further you venture into the market, the more vibrant and bohemian the blend becomes, but the darker and more intense the spiritual atmosphere.

The café was Middle Eastern in style and situated at the heart of the market, giving me a panoramic view of stalls selling food, jewellery, antiques and musical instruments from around the globe.

There were also a number of outlets for new age practices with crystals, stones, oils and religious artefacts for sale, and tarot and palm readings offered.

For whatever reason, there was a complete absence of Christian presence in this mix, and this concerned me. Was it because Christians viewed this type of setting as enemy territory? Or that the Church didn't know how to relate to such expressions of society? Or had the Christian faith been muscled out of the area? I didn't know.

Whilst puzzling over the whys and wherefores of the situation, I was confronted by a vision so powerful that I actually believed it was taking place. A line of saxophonists walked right passed the café. I couldn't hear the detail of what they were playing, just an incredible wash of sound. As they moved through the lanes of the market the atmosphere was completely transformed. A light followed them wherever they went and remained wherever they had been, so that more and more of the market began to glow. Then the Lord spoke: "Where are my musicians, Steve? Where are they?" And with that the vision dissolved right in front of my eyes.

I was in shock for a few minutes at what I had seen, but understood immediately what the Lord was saying. The musicians in the vision had been bringing the presence of God to the heart of this community. They had not been shouting, challenging or confronting the crowds about the state of their lives and the evils of society, as many Church traditions might have endorsed in the past. In fact, they hadn't used words of any kind. Instead, they had been prophesying the voice, character and life of God into the market through sound – bringing heaven to earth and transforming the very atmosphere of that place. This had been a vision of how the Church could bring powerful expressions of the Kingdom of God to any location or meeting place. It was not currently a reality.

I have been a musician for most of my life, teaching, performing and composing music in many different styles and genres, so I have long understood the concept of music as an unspoken means of communication. This is not such a revolutionary concept; composers and performers have been using music to communicate with listeners for centuries.

I have also recognised the properties of music to change moods and atmospheres, and to bring relief or healing to the human condition. On many occasions I have witnessed specific musical genres changing the atmosphere of a party or concert, and have seen at first hand the transformation music and sound therapists have brought to the lives of individuals.

During worship gatherings there have often been moments where a specific song or musical passage has transformed an entire meeting, leading to a host of prophetic words, healings and miracles. Often explained as the "arrival of the Holy Spirit" or the "manifest presence of God" – though in my experience rarely occurring without some form of anointed music – I had only ever thought of this as a chance by-product of a worship time. After experiencing the vision, however, I began to wonder whether the use of sound, intentionally focused in this way, was about to be established or re-established in the Kingdom of God. After all, the Holy Spirit can redeem just about any secular process or practice. The fact that he might wish to speak or act through music as well as through the spoken/written word, would be more of an extension of our understanding, rather than what some might consider an adoption of a new age practice.

I am not sure whether I have been paying more attention to the media in the five years since the vision, but there does appear to have been a surge of interest in the properties of sound, both in the Church and the world. A number of lectures and documentaries have been broadcast on national radio and television, and the more prophetic streams of the Church are now actively investigating how sound transforms spiritual atmosphere and changes lives. Revisiting scriptural passages with fresh eyes also seems to validate sound as a powerful tool both to create and destroy. It would therefore appear that using sound as a means of transformation and communication between heaven and earth is a rediscovery of an ancient practice, synonymous with the Kingdom of God, rather than a new discovery.

Over the ensuing five years, I set myself a quest, to research the fundamentals of prophecy, music and sound, using as much scientific, musical and biblical research and thinking as was currently available. I would then be able to draw comparisons between the essential elements of all three and discover whether the musical prophet has ever existed and if this role has a place in the world today.

This brief study is the first part of the research, where fundamental questions are asked about the nature of prophecy, music and sound, and investigations made into key biblical moments where sound has played an important role in God's redemptive plan for both individuals and communities.

1. Defining The Prophetic

The use of the term "prophetic" is widespread today. In the Kingdom, we recognise the need to be a "prophetic people". We often make gestures considered to be prophetic or move forward with our lives in a prophetic way. Time and space are given for prophecy and the prophetic in many of our meetings and encounters with God. In the world we occasionally hear a lone voice described as "prophetic", when warning of some looming disaster. In the Church, we recognise the role of the prophet often as a message-bringer, sometimes with local, national or global influence. So what do the terms prophet, prophecy and prophetic actually mean? Are there crossovers in the terminology or clear distinctions in their meaning?

In his second letter, Peter says:

"Above all, you must understand that no prophecy of Scripture came about by the prophet's own interpretation of things. For prophecy never had its origin in the human will, but prophets, though human, spoke from God as they were carried along by the Holy Spirit." (2 Peter 1:20–21)

Revelation states:

"But in the days when the seventh angel is about to sound his trumpet, the mystery of God will be accomplished, just as He announced to His servants the prophets." (Revelation 10:7)

And in Matthew:

"All this took place to fulfil what the Lord had said through the prophet: 'The virgin will conceive and give birth to a son, and they will call Him Immanuel' which means 'God with us'" (Matthew 1:22–23)

From these passages, we understand the "prophet" as *a message-bringer inspired by God through the Holy Spirit*, and "prophecy" as *the words spoken by God through a human being*. Examples of both can be found throughout Old and New Testaments, but there are distinct differences in the way both prophet and prophecy are handled in the Old and New. Old Testament prophets held an awesome and often dangerous position within the nation. They were individuals whom God had set apart to speak to kings and nations, to declare His purposes, give instructions and warnings for the immediate and distant future (some of which are yet to be fulfilled) and to call

Israel back to himself. They would also have had dealings with ordinary individuals, but the majority of written accounts detail epic deeds. The calling of Jeremiah illustrates the Old Testament prophet's role perfectly:

"The word of the Lord came to me saying, 'Before I formed you in the womb I knew you, before you were born I set you apart; I appointed you as a prophet to the nations.' 'Ah, sovereign Lord,' I said, 'I do not know how to speak; I am too young.' But the Lord said to me, 'Do not say, "I am too young." You must go to everyone I send you to and say whatever I command you. Do not be afraid of them, for I am with you and will rescue you' declares the Lord. Then the Lord reached out His hand and touched my mouth and said to me, 'I have put words in your mouth. See today I appoint you over nations and kingdoms to uproot and tear down, to destroy and overthrow, to build and to plant.'" (Jeremiah 1:4–20)

In the New Testament, there is still an awesome element to the role of the prophet, but the application of the prophetic, post-Pentecost, is far wider in range. The outpouring of the Holy Spirit potentially opened up every spiritual gift to every believer, making access to the prophetic far more universal than in the Old Testament period. Paul writes,

"Follow the way of love and eagerly desire spiritual gifts, especially the gift of prophecy. For those who speak in a tongue do not speak to other people but to God. Indeed no one understands them; they utter mysteries by the Spirit. But those who prophesy speak to people for their strengthening, encouragement and comfort. Those who speak in a tongue edify themselves, but those who prophesy edify the church. I would like every one of you to speak in tongues, but even more to prophesy." (1 Corinthians 14:1–5)

In his book, Preach the Word! Greg Haslam builds on this point:

"The New Testament, therefore teaches not only the priesthood of all believers – the watchword of the sixteenth-century European Reformation – but, as we might put it: the prophethood of all believers. In accordance with the prediction of the prophet Joel that in the last days 'I will pour out my Spirit on all flesh; and your sons and daughters shall prophesy', there is an extension on the franchise of prophetic gifts, so that their distribution crosses ageist, sexist, ethnic and social divides. The Holy Spirit is an 'equal opportunity empowerer', and the prophet Joel saw in advance this increase of prophetic in the 'last days', which competent New Testament scholarship affirms as the description of the whole era from the first to the second coming of Christ."[1]

This has huge implications for us as believers today. If "everyone" is encouraged to "desire spiritual gifts", then potentially, everyone may prophesy. Which leads us to the question: what is the main purpose of prophecy today?

Within the boundaries of edifying the Church, much of the purpose declared in Jeremiah's calling still applies. There is a time to speak to nations and kingdoms, to uproot, tear down, destroy, overthrow, build and plant. But more often today, the physical reality of the words and experiences of the Old Testament become spiritual reality in the New Testament. Therefore, unless the Lord specifically directs, he is the one who uproots, tears down, destroys and overthrows, often through our words, prayer and declarations in the Spirit, but all in the context of edifying the Church, bringing his Kingdom on earth and standing against or taking ground from the enemy.

The vast majority of prophecy for the majority of us today will take place within the body of Christ, edifying individuals, small groups, congregations or larger cross–church, area or denominational gatherings. Prophecy may deal with future events, but it is just as likely to bring elements of the unseen present to light, whether they be personal, church or community based, in order to edify those at whom they are directed.

In his book "The Prophet's Notebook", Barry Kissell writes,

"The prophetic word is charged with energy and power, and it is also effective and creative. It does what God intends it to do … The prophetic word is also living, and it has within it the power to create life – as we see at the beginning of time at the Creation: 'And God said, "Let there be light," and there was light' (Genesis 1:3)."[2]

And Greg Haslam writes,

"I am also convinced that the major work of prophetic ministry is the removal of blockages to a move of God's Spirit in our day and hour."[3]

What then is the distinction between "prophecy" and "prophetic"?

The Bible is packed full of demonstrations of the "prophetic" – messages given to individuals, nations and churches, which were often spoken, but occasionally presented in a range of creative forms: dramatic warnings, musical dialogues, symbolic marches, artistic creations. From the soothing sounds of David's harp to Jeremiah's smashed pot, Hosea's marriage to a prostitute to Ezekiel's river and measuring line, the Lord has made every effort to communicate with our whole being through every one of our senses.

So we see that the "prophetic" is therefore a collective term describing a much wider assortment of communicative acts through which God chooses to speak, going far beyond words. A working definition of the prophetic might therefore be:

"An expression of God through the words, actions or work of a human being".

Or,

"Any activity or act which brings the heart and mind of God to a situation, individual or community".

Of course, spoken prophecy belongs within this collection, but is only one of many prophetic expressions through which God has spoken and continues to speak. There are many other creative forms through which God is speaking today. Some are rediscoveries of ancient ways and truths, the principles of which are illustrated throughout the Old and New Testaments.

The arts certainly have a part to play in expressing not just the heart of Man to God, but also the heart of God to Man. For centuries music and the creative arts have been important communicative media for stirring emotion, reviving hope, awakening memory, unlocking grief and rousing passion. It would be difficult not to see them as means through which God also communicates, but how is this possible and what is it specifically about music that enables this to happen?

Endnotes

1. Greg Haslam, Preach the Word, (Sovereign World, 2006)
2. Barry Kissell, The Prophet's Notebook, (Kingsway Publications, 2002)
3. Greg Haslam, Preach the Word, (Sovereign World, 2006)

2. As David Played

"Now the Spirit of the Lord had departed from Saul, and an evil spirit from the Lord tormented him. Saul's attendants said to him 'See, an evil spirit from God is tormenting you. Let our lord command his servants here to search for someone who can play the harp. He will play when the evil spirit from God comes upon you, and you will feel better.'

So Saul said to his attendants, 'Find someone who plays well and bring him to me' One of the servants answered, 'I have seen a son of Jesse of Bethlehem who knows how to play the harp. He is a brave man and a warrior. He speaks well and is a fine-looking man. And the Lord is with him.' Then Saul sent messengers to Jesse and said 'Send me your son David, who is with the sheep.' So Jesse took a donkey loaded with bread, a skin of wine and a young goat and sent them with his son David to Saul.

David came to Saul and entered his service. Saul liked him very much and David became one of his armour-bearers. Then Saul sent word to Jesse, saying, 'Allow David to remain in my service, for I am pleased with him.' Whenever the spirit from God came upon Saul, David would take his harp and play. Then relief would come to Saul; he would feel better, and the evil spirit would leave him." (1 Samuel 16:14–23)

Have you ever read this passage and wondered what it was about David's music that was so effective in driving away an evil spirit? What did he actually play to leave Saul relieved and refreshed? David was clearly a renowned musician and a skilled warrior, but how did he actually play the harp? What did the music sound like? Was it melodic or a series of random notes? Was it harmonic or a single line melody? What rhythmic and stylistic elements did the music have? And from where did he get such dynamic and powerful ideas?

The account in 1 Samuel, like so many others in Scripture, raises questions about the role of musicians in ancient society. Were they just entertainers providing a musical backdrop to life, an accompaniment for worship, or were they much more involved in preparing for God to meet with his people?

In an earlier passage, Samuel prophesied that Saul himself would soon have a prophetic encounter:

"After that you will go to Gibeah of God, where there is a Philistine outpost. As you approach the town, you will meet a procession of prophets, coming down from the high place with lyres, tambourines, flutes and harps being played before them and they will be prophesying. The Spirit of the Lord will come upon you in power and you will prophesy with them; and you will be changed into a different person." (1 Samuel 10:5–6)

As Saul meets the prophetic company, it is interesting to note the involvement of the musicians. They were actually leading not following the prophetic group, descending from a "high place", into a town containing a dangerous enemy contingent. What exactly were they doing? What were they actually playing as they processed? Was it just a musical setting for prophecy? A morale booster as they entered enemy territory? Or could it have been a preparation for the Spirit of God to visit that place? Through this encounter, Saul was "changed into a different person".

A famous passage from Joshua raises similar questions:

"Then the Lord said to Joshua, 'See, I have delivered Jericho into your hands, along with its king and its fighting men. March around the city once with all the armed men. Do this for six days. Have seven priests carry trumpets of rams' horns in front of the ark. On the seventh day, march around the city seven times, with the priests blowing the trumpets. When you hear them sound a long blast on the trumpets, have all the people give a loud shout; then the wall of the city will collapse, and the people will go up, every man straight in.'" (Joshua 6:1–5)

What was the purpose or the symbolism in marching around the walls of the city carrying instruments for six full days before a final day of warfare? The trumpets were carried by priests "in front of" the ark rather than behind. But what did they actually play on the seventh day? Was it rhythmic? If so, did everyone play the same rhythm or did each play as they saw fit? Was there any element of melody or harmony involved, or was the sound a deliberate cacophony to instil terror in the city? Did the trumpeters breathe together when playing or stagger their breathing to create one continuous sound? Did anyone lead or coordinate the musicians? And how was the "long blast" orchestrated?

In many respects, questions regarding Old Testament instruments are hypothetical when their sound quality is compared with today's standards. But each of the passages questions the role of musicians and the music they played at key moments in biblical history – and at key outpourings of God's mercy, anointing and power. Passages such as these also question the role and significance of music and musicians in the Church today.

The whole of human history has been punctuated by moves of God upon his Church as he restores the fullness of his Kingdom to earth. From recognition of the need for personal salvation to the restoration of the gifts of the Holy Spirit, God has been progressively restoring fundamental beliefs and outworkings of the Spirit, both reviving and restoring his bride to become all she was meant to be.

During this current season of renewal and empowering, God appears to be restoring much of the supernatural and miraculous absent from the Church for centuries. New areas of ministry, which previous generations of believers may not have understood, are thriving. Burn 24-7[1], Healing on the Streets[2], Healing Rooms[3] and Treasure Hunting[4] are just some of the ministries touching both believers and unbelievers across the nations. The interpretation of dreams and visions and Bethel Sozo[5] prayer sessions are radically transforming the prophetic input and output of individuals. Listening to God and praying in line with what he is saying, rather than presenting him with a shopping list, is beginning to bring the Church more into line with his divine will.

Worship too appears to be to radically changing in focus, taking more of a prime place in meetings, allowing a divine exchange between God and Man, rather than serving purely as a preparation for the "Word" or prayer ministry. Individuals are being restored to wholeness as the Father embraces his Church. His sovereignty, power and love are moving into the lives of his children more permanently, reviving them, restoring their hope and blessing them in abundance.

God is pouring out his Spirit across the earth like never before, and the weight of his presence is being felt by communities of believers everywhere. Through soaking times and encounter meetings, God is revealing ancient truths and uncapping resources to fulfil his promises and reveal his love. In so doing, he is reminding us that he is more than able to speak to his people without a priest or mediator. As we break out in worship creatively, where to dance, paint or play our instruments prophetically is just a starting point, we realise he is not limited to using voices or vocabulary to reach into people's lives.

So how does this impact the way we lead worship in our times together or the way in which we play our instruments as musicians? In many respects, our foundations are secure. A heart worshipping God in Spirit and in truth may do so in any style, and in any format. Words and music written from the heart by men and women across the centuries will always find a resonance with those worshipping centuries later. But as cultures change and God restores truth and brings new things, so then our understanding and expressions also need to change. The wineskin of our corporate meetings needs to be restored in truth and the way we interact with the rest of the world made new.

Endnotes

For further information on these ministries, visit the following websites:

1. www.burn24-7.com
2. www.healingonthestreets.org
3. www.healingrooms.com
4. www.ibethel.org/treasure-hunts
5. www.bethelsozo.com

3. Every Song Has A Spirit

Every piece of music that has ever been written, composed or improvised has a spirit. This is not just a Christian phenomenon. All music, by its very nature, creates atmosphere and conveys some emotion which demands an internal or external response from the listener. Listen to a Wagner overture or a Coldplay song and you will perceive the emotion or spirit intended by the composer, or through the interpretation given by its performer. Watch a heavy metal or Motown concert and you will discern very different atmospheres brought about by the messages of each musical style.

Communication is at the heart of every piece of music, whether or not the piece has words. Through melody, harmony and rhythm, choice of genre, instrumentation, timbres and textures, a whole package of messages is delivered to the listener in both classical and popular styles. Our first response as listeners is whether we like or dislike what we hear and then, almost involuntarily, thoughts, memories and emotions are inspired and released.

Music is intrinsically emotional and spiritual. It makes sense of who we are as human beings, using sound in the same way that dance uses movement and art uses form and visual stimuli. Creative arts inspire us to connect with the unseen, forcing us to engage with feelings locked deep within and with the spiritual world around us.

Current research by physicists suggests that the smallest elements of life itself consist not of atoms but of sound particles or "strings" 100 times smaller than the atom[1], confirming sound as a primary creative force. With sound as its key component, therefore, music not only enriches our existence, adding beauty and dimension to life, but also gives us the creative power to communicate with the rest of the human race and with God, should we choose to do so.

Imagine then if God himself became the instigator in communicating with us through music, expressing his heart not just through the words of a prophet, but also through those involved in the creative arts.

Even if we rarely communicate anything original musically with others, our ability to communicate with ourselves through what we hear is phenomenal. Memory, imagination and spiritual awareness all play a significant role in this process, and there are a number of musical genres designed deliberately to focus the mind in this way. In the secular world, for example, there are countless forms of both classical and popular music which allow us to be influenced by the composer's own thoughts and feelings. Programme music relies heavily on the imagination to visualise a story being told musically. Opera invites us to partake in the raw emotion of the players on stage. Ambient electronic music encourages us to relax. The vocal lines of soul music call us to love our fellow human beings.

In the Kingdom too there are many musical styles which encourage us to worship in very different ways. Hymns can reflect the greatness of God and the depths of his love, often confirming doctrines or beliefs within their verses, whilst simple choruses may emphasise the intimacy of his relationship with us. Upbeat gospel songs or rock anthems bring out the dancer or rejoicer, whilst solo incidental music performed on organ or piano encourages reflection. "Soaking" music too, often grander in its timescale than the average congregational worship session, brings a spirit of insight and relaxation into God's presence, whilst "harp and bowl" intercessory worship engages us deeply in prayer.

Worship, however, is a two way process. In his book, Exploring Worship, Bob Sorge writes,

"Worship has always been ordained of God to be more than a monologue of my telling him how I feel about him. Worship is more than just my talking to God – it is also his talking to me! Worship is an exchange – it is two-way communication.

Worship has been called the 'language of love'. When we worship, we express our love to God. But love must flow as an exchange between two individuals. There must be give and take, talking and listening, transmitting and receiving. When I love my wife, I do not go on and on about my feelings for her, nor do I occupy the conversation exclusively with my own opinion and feelings. I give her an opportunity to respond, allowing her to give expression to her own inner emotions.

Worship must contain both elements in order to be complete; it must consist of our expressions unto God, and then it must also include listening to his responses."[2]

So as God visits our institutions and gatherings and inhabits our churches more permanently, the very nature of how we do Kingdom business appears to be changing, along with the partnership dynamic between God and ourselves. Shopping list prayer, one-way directional worship, the way we pray for healing or deal with strongholds are being turned on their heads. Through the use of the creative in areas such as soaking, interpretation of dreams and Bethel Sozo, God is reviving a whole host of supernatural ministries which rely on listening to him first before we begin to speak out vocally.

Music is an essential part of this new season. It is taking its place amongst creative arts being revived by God as a prophetic means through which he can speak directly or indirectly to individuals, communities and nations. But how does prophesying on a musical instrument work in practice? Does "prophetic music" have a unique role in the body of Christ or is it just another way

of reinforcing spoken prophecy? How does God speak to us
through music and are "prophetic music" and "musical prophet"
valid terms?

Endnotes

1. Information on String and Superstring theory can be found on "The
Official String Theory Web Site":
www.superstringtheory.com
2. Bob Sorge, Exploring Worship, (Oasis House, 1987)

4. Recognising The Power Of Music

Music is often described as a universal language, playing a central role in virtually every culture on earth. From a mother singing her child to sleep to a music therapist reconnecting dementia sufferers with their past, music takes a prime position in the physical, mental and spiritual wellbeing of most individuals.

Music also has a key role in our collective consciousness. Whether in grief expressed through songs at a funeral or in the jubilation of a football chant, music creates a common identity, a shared experience fundamental to the expression of humanity. The philosopher Plato wrote:

"Music gives a soul to the universe, wings to the mind, flight to the imagination and life to everything."[1]

His epic work "The Republic" devotes just one paragraph to economics, but forty pages to music.

The opening and closing ceremonies of the London 2012 Olympics were a potent symbol of the power of music to capture the heart and mind of a nation. Both events were highly charged with a variety of musical styles creating atmosphere and demanding emotional participation. Whether playing an instrument, singing or listening, music fosters a shared dynamic rarely experienced in any other way, but how exactly does music identify and change the human condition?

Science has made a number of discoveries over the past four decades confirming the influence of music on the mind and body, which many musicians and scientists have intuitively felt for centuries. At the same time, biblical scholars have been unearthing hidden meaning in texts which allude or directly refer to music's emotional and spiritual impact on our daily lives.

The brain

Recent technological advances have enabled scientists to monitor brain activity when exposed to a variety of stimuli. Music has been shown specifically to create a range of emotions in those engaged in any form of activity, whether listening, playing or singing. The music that we enjoy arouses strong emotional responses which flood the brain with blood releasing dopamine, a chemical promoting a sense of pleasure and well being. Where this occurs, MRI scans show intense activity in the deepest recesses of the brain in the same measure as when needs such as thirst, hunger and even love are met. Such is the need for music in the life of an individual. Though the musical styles and pieces we dislike arouse very different emotions, personal engagement in them is limited and therefore far less brain activity registers.

Both hearing and playing music stimulates emotion, usually provoking a reaction:

• Modifying or producing a specific pattern of behaviour
• Promoting mental stimulation
• Bringing a spiritual revelation which may lead to an encounter with God

Emotion promotes response. Tears, laughter and longing may all be aroused through music, but choices, behaviour patterns and courses of action may also follow: the need to spend time thinking, for example, or to declare one's love for another human being, or to identify with the emotion through dance or song.

Advertising agencies have long realised the potential music has to inspire interest in a product. Shopping malls use specific musical styles to foster the desire to spend money and other styles to repel groups involved in anti-social behaviour or crime. Nightclubs create an ambience for dance through a mix of specific tunes and then signal when it is time to leave at the end of the evening through others.

Emotions aroused through music also promote mental stimulation and creativity. Research has shown that playing or listening to music engages a number of unique areas in the brain and many links between them. Memory is inspired through music, which is why the lyrics to a song are so much easier to memorise than the words of a poem or a set of facts and figures. But music also stirs thought and creativity. Children who play a musical instrument or listen to specific types of classical music are proven to have a general level of aptitude and ability greater than those who do not.[2] Einstein, a very able violinist, said:

"If I were not a physicist, I would probably be a musician. I often think in music. I live my daydreams in music. I see my life in terms of music."[3]

When discussing a particular breakthrough in his work, he made the following observation:

"It occurred to me by intuition, and music was the driving force behind that intuition. My discovery was the result of musical perception."[4]

The English term "music" is thought by some to have been derived from the Greek "mousike", an art form presided over by the "Muses", Greek goddesses who were believed to promote thought in literature, science and the arts. This philosophy lay at the heart of the social and spiritual culture of Ancient Greece and led to the development of the verb "to muse" and the noun "music". The link between music and thought has therefore been recognised for thousands of years.

Emotion aroused through music can often bring a spiritual encounter or revelation. Beethoven said, "Music is a higher revelation than all wisdom and philosophy ... Music is the mediator between spiritual and sensual life."[5]

There is a heavenly link between God and Man in music. Elisha was enabled to bring a word from the Lord when the minstrel played. David brought mental relief and refreshment to Saul when he prophesied through the harp, and the men sent to capture David encountered God as they approached the company of prophets surrounding him. Martin Luther recognised this in the 16th Century. He wrote,

"Music is a fair and glorious gift of God. I am strongly persuaded that after theology, there is no art which can be placed on the level with music. The devil flees before the sound of music almost as much as before the word of God."[6]

In fact, music can promote higher levels of spirituality, thought and behaviour across a town, city or nation. Damon of Athens, a musicologist and contemporary of Plato said,

"Give me the songs of a nation, and I care not who makes its laws."[7]

In a 17th Century echo of this sentiment, Blaise Pascal, the French mathematician, physicist and Christian philosopher, observed that the people who have the greatest influence in shaping the hearts and minds of a society or impacting a generation are not those who write its laws, but those who write its songs.

Indeed, the music expressed by individuals or a community often does reflect their inner state of mind and spirit. In a lecture given to the Sacred Arts Foundation in 2009, Peter Kreeft, Professor of Philosophy at The King's College, New York, related the legend of a Chinese emperor who made practical use of this theory:

"There was a Chinese emperor who, according to legend, ran China by music for about forty years … He didn't have many soldiers. And there was a civil war breaking out all over the place. He disguised himself as a peasant and visited each of his … major cities once a year, walking through the streets and listening to the music that the people sang and played. And if the music was in harmony with the Tao – the way of the universe, of nature, and of sanctity in a human life – he would let it alone. But if the music was disharmonious and expressed antagonism to the Tao – he was sensitive to that – he would go back to his capital and send soldiers to that city, who would then be on hand when the revolt broke out a month later."

Rhythm

Rhythm is a fundamental element of music. It plays a key role in the stimulation of the brain and our enjoyment of certain musical styles. Rhythm is also fundamental to the development of language, society and health.

Experiments have shown that the brain is particularly wired for rhythm and that there are close links between the brain's sound and motor systems. Babies of six months old are more than able to respond to rhythm without assistance from their parents, moving in time to a beat and displaying an ability to anticipate what happens next rhythmically. Response and anticipation such as this is thought to be linked to the development of language, confirming rhythm as a fundamental part of human development. Response to a number of musical styles which rely heavily on rhythmic patterns and emphatic bass lines such as "dub step" and several rave genres prove this ability is not lost as we grow older.

Recognition and anticipation of beat also create opportunities for shared experience. In areas such as dance and musical appreciation, recognising a beat almost always creates a response, whether nodding the head, tapping a foot, clicking the fingers or analysing the beat internally. When two people recognise, appreciate and anticipate the same musical material, the chance to play, sing or dance together is created.

Therapy and health

Rhythm therapy is part of a wealth of developing practices designed to improve the lives of those who need rehabilitation or are suffering physical or mental health conditions.

For thirty years, a hospital in New York has been pioneering the therapeutic powers of rhythm to treat sufferers of Parkinson's disease. Parkinson's creates difficulties in the coordination of movement and balance of patients due to the number of lost nerve cells. Dopamine produced by the nerve cells is essential for both movement and balance. A lack of this chemical can also result in patients suffering uncontrollable shakes or a complete freeze of movement. Dr Concetta Tomaino[8] of the Institute for Music and Neurologic Function, New York, uses music with a strong rhythm to remedy the deficit within the brain, helping patients to balance correctly and move more fluidly. The treatment bypasses the brain's damaged areas helping to drive its motor function. Though each patient reacts quite differently to treatment, dramatic effects are felt almost immediately. Therapy is not limited to use of rhythm, though. A mother singing her child to sleep or a nursery nurse playing or performing music during a pre-schoolers' afternoon rest time is just as much a part of therapy as professional provision.

Music therapy is established as a professional practice across the world, using every possible impact or musical association to bring wholeness to individuals living with a variety of conditions and circumstances. There are thousands of organisations each with their own area of expertise, philosophy and working practices. The following use similar methods to provide services to two very different user groups:

Nordorff Robbins[9] is a leading provider of music therapy in the UK, working with a variety of ages and conditions at care homes, day centres, hospitals and schools to improve physical health and ability, address emotional and behavioural difficulties, develop communication and social skills and increase creativity, self-esteem and confidence. Musicians work with the chronically and terminally ill, those with learning difficulties or autistic spectrum disorders, those affected with physical or sensory impairment and those suffering with dementia.

Changing Tunes[10] is a leading provider of rehabilitation through music for prisoners and ex-prisoners in the UK, using music teaching, rehearsing, performing, improvising and composing to befriend, build self-esteem, educate, assist and change attitudes of offenders. Rehabilitation sessions provided in this way give prisoners the role models, supportive relationships, opportunities and stability they have missed throughout much of their lives. Support is continued on release providing the ex-prisoner with a much greater chance of becoming part of the wider community and remaining within the law.

Organisations such as these are typical of thousands of others which give opportunities to communicate to those who, through a variety of reasons have difficulty expressing themselves vocally or verbally, making more sense of the lives they live.

In the story of David and Saul, David's playing brought health and healing to the mind, body and spirit. Saul was refreshed in his mind, made well in his body and the evil spirit left him. In both the Old and New Testaments, we often see evil spirits as the cause of illness. In this particular case, the harp appeared to have a resonance to cure and deliver Saul. Quite remarkably today, a growing number of hospitals across the United States are actually employing harpists to play in operating theatres during heart operations. It would appear that scientists are beginning to discover the harp's healing qualities, the resonance of the harp strings appearing to sooth the heart and regulate quivering heart rhythms.[11]

In Old Testament times, according to Dr Amnon Shiloah,[12] the world's leading authority on Arab and Jewish music traditions, ancient texts describe how doctors should use music to treat their patients. They also detail when a music expert, minstrel or other live performer should be called to assist them. Accounts are given of the Ten Commandments or specific psalms being prescribed to be sung in a specific mode or scale to bring healing from specific illnesses.

The ramifications of music as a universal language and its potential power in both the Kingdom of God and society at large appear to go far deeper than most of us realise.

Endnotes

1. There are many available translations of this classic. This one: Plato and Robin Waterfield, The Republic, (Oxford Paperbacks; New Ed. Edition, 2008).

2. The power of music to increase intellectual ability and patterns of behaviour is discussed in The Mozart Effect, Don Campbell (Quill, Reprint edition, 2001).

3. Dan McCollam, God Vibrations: A Christian perspective on the power of sound (DVD Teaching Series produced through the Institute for Worship and Arts Resources by Sound Wisdom Media).

4. Ibid.

5. Ibid.

6. Ibid.

7. Ibid.

8. Dr Concetta M. Tomaino, D.A., MT-BC, LCAT Executive Director/ Co-Founder, Institute for Music and Neurologic Function, New York. Website: www.musictherapy.imnf.org

9. For further information on Nordorff Robbins visit: www.nordorff-robbins.org.uk

10. For further information on Changing Tunes visit: www.changingtunes.org.uk

11. Research taking place in hospitals such as Morristown Medical Centre, New Jersey, and the Carle Heart Center, Urbana, Illinois, is available online. Introductory articles can be found at:

www.empowereddoctor.com/hearts-and-harps

www.highstrangeness.tv/0-1541-harp-music-in-hospital-is-surreal-and-heals-html

12. Dr Amnon Shiloah, Professor (Emeritus) of Musicology at the Hebrew University of Jerusalem.

5. Understanding The Power Of Sound

Resonant Frequency

The whole universe is built on the principles of sound. Physics teaches us that all matter vibrates. Vibration of any kind produces a frequency and frequency is the universal currency of sound.

Frequency is measured in hertz (Hz), that is the number of vibrations or oscillations per second. The height or depth of the sound produced is determined by the speed of the vibration. The higher the number or hertz the higher the sound.

Frequency applies to every natural and man-made object on earth, and every star, planet and asteroid in the universe. The earth itself vibrates at between 6 and 10Hz. Light too exists as vibration, but around 21 times higher than any audible frequency. The colour spectrum represents a whole range of different frequencies, each colour oscillating at a different speed.

The principles of sound are right at the heart of understanding life itself. Scientists are currently investigating a number of theories on how the universe holds together. String and Superstring theory[1] attempt to redefine our understanding of the atom as a particle made of tiny vibrating lines or "strings" – a departure from any previous atomic theory. Research, the emergence of such theories, and a greater understanding of sound itself are beginning to confirm aspects of the biblical accounts of the creation of the universe:

"In the beginning God created the heavens and the earth. Now the earth was formless and empty, darkness was over the surface of the deep and the *spirit* of God was *hovering* over the waters. And God *said*, 'Let there be *light*,' and there was light." (Genesis 1:1–3)

The Hebrew word for "spirit" in this passage, ruach, is used to describe any type of spirit, wind or breath, hence the qualification "of God". "Hovering" is a translation of merachefet, used in only one other biblical passage (Deuteronomy 32:11) to describe an eagle's fluttering motion as she circulates air over her eggs. This implies that the Holy Spirit was moving rapidly to and fro over the earth in a fluttering, vibratory manner. Then God spoke and light, a supersonic frequency, became earth's first visible formation.

The opening of John's gospel clarifies this:

"In the beginning was the Word, and the Word was with God, and the Word was God. He was with God in the beginning. Through Him all things were made; without Him nothing was made that has been made. In Him was life, and that life was the light of all people. The light shines in the darkness and the darkness has not overcome it." (John 1:1–5)

John states categorically that Jesus Christ is the word of God and all things were made through him. Although there was a three-way partnership involved in the creation of the universe, Jesus was the word that brought formation to all things. Colossians builds on this truth:

"For in Him, all things were created: things in heaven and on earth, visible and invisible, whether thrones or powers or rulers or authorities; all things have been created through Him and for Him. He is before all things and in Him all things hold together." (Colossians 1:16–17)

As Jesus was the word that spoke all things into existence through the breath of God and the power of the Holy Spirit, he is the one who holds the universe together through the power of the very sound which spoke creation into being. Everything on earth and across the universe therefore vibrates at the frequency of the voice of God, and it is this very voice which continues to hold it together. This is not just a figurative passage; scientists are actually beginning to discover it as truth.

An understanding of these very principles will have dynamic repercussions for every believer, especially those involved in the creation or production of any type of music or sound. Firstly, imagine how close Jesus is to us on a daily basis if his voice is the force which holds all things together surrounding us. Even the chair I am sitting on has a frequency which emanates his original command.

Secondly, if sound is the driving and binding force behind creation and we are the expression of the will and love of God on earth, imagine the potential in imitating that original command, coming into line with the principles set out in creation. The power to create, to bind together, to bring order out of chaos and even to destroy where necessary through sound must surely resonate with the principles of heaven. The writer of Proverbs understood this principle in relation to the voice:

"The tongue has power of life and death, and those who love it will eat its fruit." (Proverbs 18:21)

There are a significant number of other passages throughout Scripture which confirm and demonstrate this principle.

Of course, though frequencies exist all around us, they are rarely heard in their own right. Occasionally, a surface or object will cause another to vibrate and a sound is heard, but more usually, the surface or object will need to be struck in some way in order to hear the sound it produces. If we think of the strings of a piano, each one is tuned to a specific pitch, but they are not heard until the piano's hammers strike them. The same principles apply to objects such as the wine glass, which vibrates in the same way as all other matter, but needs to be tapped to hear the tone it produces. The sound inherent in the glass is prolonged when tapped, making it resonate. The technical term for this sound is *resonant frequency*.

It is resonant frequency which gives an object, musical instrument or voice its purpose and power in the same way that light could only fulfil its purpose as God spoke it into being. At that point it ceased to be a theory and became a reality. The sound of the harp in 1 Samuel 16 was able to bring relief to Saul on many levels, but until David actually played the strings allowing those sounds to be heard, the harp could not fulfil its purpose.

We see in the accounts of Creation and observations made in previous chapters how sound and music (organised sound) are used as both creative and binding forces. The earth was made through the word of God, which also holds it together; music creates atmospheres in which humans interact positively with one another and into which God can speak; music can change the human condition creating possibilities which thwart the onset of both physical and mental illness. Both sound and music can also bring order out of chaos. Music trains the mind and focuses thought. It is also fundamental in the formation of language, and was able to transform Saul's life into physical, mental and spiritual health. Sound also brought order into the world which was described as "formless" until God spoke. Dan McCollam[2] in his teaching series "God Vibrations"[3] takes the demonstration of this reality one stage further.

Using a chladni plate[4] randomly sprinkled with sand, a series of sounds, frequencies and pitches are passed through the plate, bringing a visible order to the sand, forming perfectly structured patterns, each a unique representation of a voice, instrument or random object. McCollam calls this "inanimate matter scrambling to take the shape of the sound that was introduced to it", a representation of the Genesis account of creation. He repeats this experiment with a Rubens tube[5], a tube with a line of holes into which flame is forced. This time a variety of musical styles and pieces are played through the tube creating patterns in the flames, a visualisation of the sound waves created through each musical piece.

Though sound is a powerful creative and binding force, however, it also has the capacity to destroy.

Entrainment

Entrainment is a universal concept applying to physics, mathematics, physical geography, physiology, engineering and a number of other sciences.

Referring to its application in physics, Dan McCollam describes entrainment as, "the tendency of two oscillating bodies to lock into phase." In other words, two objects with the same resonant frequency will eventually lock together into sequence.

The process of entrainment was discovered by the Dutch physicist and inventor of the pendulum clock, Christian Huygens, in 1665. He noticed that the pendulums of two identical clocks hanging next to each other always synchronised perfectly in an identical or 1800 opposite direction. No matter how many times the pendulums were swung out of phase, they would eventually lock back into one of these synchronised patterns. More recent discoveries have shown that entrainment is the result of small amounts of energy transferring from one object to another, amounts becoming less and less until the objects are in total phase with each other.

Entrainment has both creative and destructive properties. Heart pacemakers use entrainment to operate effectively. Dance uses the principles of entrainment both consciously and subconsciously to synchronise movement between two or more people through the recognition of a beat. The Bible too alludes to entrainment in its promotion of discipleship, in assuming the yoke of Jesus and avoiding being yoked together with unbelievers. The principle of marriage, of two becoming one flesh also implies a form of entrainment. The "Thy kingdom come, thy will be done on earth as it is in heaven" section of the Lord's Prayer is also surely founded on the principle of entrainment, the synchronisation of hearts and society with the resonance and heartbeat of heaven. However, the principal properties of entrainment most recognised today, and in both world and biblical history, are those of destruction.

The locking into phase of two objects with the same resonant frequency can have potentially explosive results for one of those objects. When a frequency is aimed at an object with an identical resonant frequency, it will be forced to vibrate in entrainment with that frequency. The object on the receiving end will be weakened and eventually destroyed. The louder and longer the frequency, the more violently it will be forced to vibrate and the quicker the destruction.

To visualise this, imagine a wine glass. The glass has a frequency which resonates when it is tapped. If you direct the exact frequency of the wine glass towards the glass itself using a tone generator or a voice, the molecules of the glass will be forced to come into entrainment with the frequency being produced and will begin to vibrate. The longer and louder the sound source, the more violently the molecules will vibrate, until the glass is unable to keep up with the vibration and will shatter.

This is a well known phenomenon and is often associated with opera singers and their ability to shatter glass. However, realistically, the voice is not often as precise or powerful for long enough to enable this to happen. Entrainment is not a random action. Glasses and other objects do not break simply because of an identical resonant frequency somewhere in the area. Entrainment takes consistency, aim, direction, focus and precision. There is little chance of a random occurrence of entrainment bringing destruction. However, in a number of exceptional circumstances, disasters have occurred.

Soon after the opening of the Tacoma Narrows Bridge, Washington State, in July 1940 the bridge began to sway violently from side to side. As a result it was given the nickname "Gallopin' Gertie". By November of the same year the mile long suspension bridge had collapsed. Footage of the incident is available from a number of sources. On investigation, the disaster was not caused by the force of the wind which regularly whipped through the Pass spanned by the bridge, but its effect on the bridge's cables. The wind caused the cables to vibrate at a resonant frequency identical to that of the concrete and steel of the rest of the bridge. Although the frequency was very low and impossible to hear with the human ear, the bridge came into entrainment with the cables for long enough to set up a powerful vibration. The molecules of the bridge attempted to match the frequency of the cables which resulted in the bridge's eventual collapse. Video footage shows the architect of the bridge attempting to stabilise the situation by driving his car to the centre of the bridge. However, the car was of insufficient weight and mass to prevent the disaster. As a result of this collapse, acoustic engineers were involved in all subsequent building projects.

Several bridges in England have faced similar problems. In 1831 the Broughton Suspension Bridge in Manchester collapsed as soldiers marched in formation across it. By marching in step with each other the regular pattern they were creating produced the exact frequency of the bridge itself, setting up entrainment and destroying the bridge. From that day, the British Army ordered that troops should always break step when crossing a bridge.

A similar incident took place in 2000 on the Millennium Bridge, which links the Tate Modern Gallery with St Pauls Cathedral in London. The bridge, built for pedestrians began to sway from the minute it opened. Though pedestrians were not marching in step, entrainment began to work on two levels.

Firstly, the same principles of beat recognition which synchronise individuals on a dance floor have a similar effect in city centres. Beat and rhythm unite, so that a general resonance and locking into phase of pedestrians walking begins to build regular step patterns. The difference between a city centre and a bridge is one of concentration and direction. Pedestrians in a city centre have many destinations covering a wide area. On a bridge, ground area, direction and speed are far more concentrated, which causes powerful patterns to emerge as in this case.

A second level of entrainment began to take place on the Millennium Bridge as step/beat patterns affected the bridge's resonant frequency. Thankfully, architects took early action and the bridge was closed for two years to correct the design flaws.

Bridges are not the only structures affected by entrainment. There are stories of cathedral bell towers and skyscrapers beginning to shake, caused by resonant frequencies or music creating entrainment patterns. There is even a theory that the rapid collapse of the twin towers in the terrorist attacks of 2001 in New York was due not just to the damage caused by the initial collision or burning aviation fuel, but because each jet had struck the tubular construction of the towers, causing them to vibrate. This would have set up a resonance which resulted in entrainment, bringing total devastation.

Spiritual Awareness

Cracking a wine glass takes aim, direction, determined focus and precision. Though the bridge incidents of Tacoma, Manchester and London were not the result of deliberate sabotage, the same conditions were unintentionally created.

Sound is a phenomenally powerful force and part of God's plan to demolish demonic strongholds in the lives of individuals and communities across the world, through the resonance of worship and intentionally created sound directed prophetically into situations and areas of conflict, pain and darkness. Imagine the principle of power directed in ultrasound treatment to shatter kidney and gall stones applied to the body, mind and spirit situations of individuals, cities and nations. Such prophetic and directional use of sound could tackle longstanding spiritual issues, stubborn mental and physical health problems, displace occupying territorial spirits, principalities and powers, counter enemy attacks, change spiritual atmospheres and maintain air supremacy in spiritual realms.

The Bible is full of accounts where sound plays a major part in the victory of a nation (usually the Israelites) and the downfall of another. In Joshua 6, the Israelites are commanded to,

"March around the city once with all the armed men. Do this for six days … On the seventh day, march around the city seven times, with the priests blowing the trumpets."

The Israelites were involved in focused marching near the walls of the city for six days, setting up a pattern of obedience to God, listening for further instruction and no doubt bringing terror to the city's inhabitants. Then on the seventh day they were to:

"…march around the city seven times, with the priests blowing the trumpets. When you hear them sound a long blast on the trumpets, have all the people give a loud shout; then the wall of the city will collapse, and the people will go up, every man straight in."

Not only was entrainment set up through marching, but also the blast of the trumpets and the shouting would almost certainly have matched the resonant frequency of the fabric of the city, causing a powerful vibration which would have totally destroyed the city walls. This was a combination of the processes which destroyed both the Broughton Suspension Bridge in Manchester and the Tacoma Narrows Bridge in Washington. Of course, God was on the move with the Israelites and there was obvious angelic involvement. Joshua is in no doubt as to who brought the victory:

"The seventh time round, when the priests sounded the trumpet blast, Joshua commanded the army, 'Shout! For the Lord has given you this city!'" (Joshua 6:16)

However, the process and the victory were a supernatural partnership between the Lord and the Israelites using principles set in place at Creation.

In 2 Samuel, the Lord uses sound to indicate to David when he should act:

"Once more the Philistines came up and spread out in the Valley of Rephaim; so David enquired of the Lord, and he answered, 'Do not go straight up, but circle round behind them and attack them in front of the poplar trees. As soon as you hear the sound of marching in the tops of the poplar trees, move quickly, because that will mean the Lord has gone out in front of you to strike the Philistine army.'" (2 Samuel 5:22–24)

In 2 Kings the Lord uses sound to rout the enemy. At a time of great famine, three lepers decide to surrender themselves to the Aramean enemy. They were starving and had nothing to lose. When they arrived at the Aramean camp, it was deserted:

"At dusk they got up and went to the camp of the Arameans. When they reached the edge of the camp, no one was there, for the Lord had caused the Arameans to hear the sound of chariots and horses and a great army, so they said to one another, 'Look, the king of Israel has hired the Hittite and Egyptian kings to attack us!' So they got up and fled in the dusk and abandoned their tents and horses and donkeys. They left the camp as it was and ran for their lives." (2 Kings 7:5–7)

In the 1970s, a number of governments began to develop sonic weapons programmes. The result was a group of highly effective directional devices which could stun both individuals and groups of people or suggest events were taking place such as car crashes or vicious dogs approaching. Frequencies were also developed to cause immediate bodily discomfort such as the "brown note" which could instantly bring on a diarrhoea attack and a range of other frequencies designed to cause pain in specific organs of the body. Specific frequency ranges could cause two people in a room to turn on each other violently or an individual to self harm or mutilate. In the "God Vibrations" teaching programme, Dan McCollam draws comparisons with biblical accounts of what appear to be sonic warfare:

"After consulting the people, Jehosophat appointed men to sing to the Lord and to praise him for the splendour of his holiness as they went out at the head of the army, saying: 'Give thanks to the Lord, for his love endures forever.' As they began to sing and praise, the Lord set ambushes against the men of Ammon and Moab and Mount Seir who were invading Judah, and they were defeated. The Ammonites and Moabites rose up against the men from Mount Seir to destroy and annihilate them. After they finished slaughtering the men from Seir, they helped to destroy one another. When the men of Judah came to the place that overlooks the desert and looked towards the vast army, they saw only dead bodies lying on the ground; no one had escaped." (2 Chronicles 20:21–24)

Two tribes fought against the third as the Israelites sang, and then the remaining two destroyed each other. McCollam calls this the "breaker anointing" which releases power against the enemy, destroying them without raising a hand.

The same principles apply in the passage we read in Acts 16 chapter 5 regarding Paul and Silas, who changed the atmosphere of the prison they had been thrown into by choosing to worship the Lord. The results were dramatic.

Using the principles of sound to bring a powerful anointing or the "breaker anointing", is nothing new or new age. It is simply a reconnection with an ancient understanding of the principles set in place as part of the process of Creation.

Hearing

Hearing can be defined as the conduction of sound waves to the brain. It takes place in two ways:

- **Air conduction** through the ear – sound waves move through the auditory canal and middle ear to the inner ear which causes pressure on the ear drum. The ear interprets this pressure as sound and sends messages to the brain.

- **Bone conduction** through the body's skeletal system – sound waves travel through the body's skeletal system to bones of the skull and the inner ear. The ear interprets this sound and sends messages to the brain.

Hearing plays a central role in human experience, affecting body, mind and spirit. Its function impacts our lives enormously and is at least partly responsible for who we are. The human ear typically picks up frequencies between 20 and 20,000Hz, though individuals vary and the older one becomes the narrower the range. Inventors have cashed in on this knowledge producing a device which emits a high-pitched frequency which only the young can hear. Shopkeepers are able to install the device to keep gangs of loitering teenagers from their premises. Some school children have used this principle, installing high-pitched ring tones on their mobiles, which teachers are unable to hear, thus allowing them to use their phones in class.

The voices we listen to and the sounds we hear contribute significantly to the development of both our character and belief system. The words of a song, the emotion inherent in a musical style, the general chit chat of the group we hang out with, the listening environment we experienced as a child and a host of other listening events develop our understanding and inner direction. Auditory nerves in the ear make numerous connections to the brain providing a super highway to the mind, spirit and body. As the experience of Saul testifies, what we hear can truly change our lives for better or for worse.

"So then, faith comes by hearing, and hearing by the word of God." (Romans 10:17 NKJV)

However, we are not only affected by the sounds and words of others, but by our own. When we direct sound towards other individuals, groups or situations the sounds we produce will also resonate and take form in our own minds and bodies. This not only defines purpose and character to those listening, but also confirms the same in us. "Death and life are in the power of the tongue" (Proverbs 18:21 NKJV). Therefore, as we choose to create or destroy through the sounds we make, those very sounds will also resonate through our own auditory and skeletal system in the same way as those to whom they are directed.

We can equally curse or bless our own minds, hearts and bodies through what we say and the sounds we make to others.

"My son, pay attention to what I say; turn your ear to my words. Do not let them out of your sight, keep them within your heart; for they are life to those who find them and health to one's whole body. Above all else, guard your heart, for everything you do flows from it. Keep your mouth free of perversity; keep corrupt talk far from your lips." (Proverbs 4:20–24)

Bones are tremendous conductors of sound. Being fibrous they vibrate with every sound directed towards us or those we make ourselves. We literally resonate with everything we say and when someone else speaks into our lives, especially at close proximity, our bones vibrate with every word.

Once again, the power of life and death in what we receive affects us significantly. The book of Proverbs is particularly helpful in this matter:

"Gracious words are a honeycomb, sweet to the soul and healing to the bones." (Proverbs 16:24)

"Light in a messenger's eyes brings joy to the heart, and good news gives health to the bones." (Proverbs 15:30)

"A cheerful heart is good medicine, but a crushed spirit dries up the bones." (Proverbs 17:22)

It is also significant that the ears and bones are linked in maintaining the body's physical balance mechanisms, as well as being the gateway for spiritual and moral balance.

"The words of a gossip are like choice morsels; they go down to the inmost parts." (Proverbs 18:8)

"A heart at peace gives life to the body, but envy rots the bones." (Proverbs 14:30)

McCollam gives examples in his teaching of people who have arthritis or osteoporosis identifying themselves as those who have had negative words, curses or death spoken repeatedly over their lives. Through forgiveness, the breaking of curses and replacement with positive prophetic words, the spirit of love and life gradually replaces the spirit of hate and death in their lives and many of them are healed of their conditions.

It is vital, therefore, that we learn to interpret what we hear, and to control what we say and the sounds we produce. The Bible refers to this as guarding your heart and mind:

"Above all else, guard your heart, for everything you do flows from it." (Proverbs 4:23)

"And do not be conformed to this world, but be transformed by the renewing of your mind, that you may prove what is that good and acceptable and perfect will of God." (Romans 12:2 NKJV)

Sound has the same power and authority to bring life and death as the tongue. The vocal inflection of a sentence needs no words or understanding of language for the listener to understand the spirit or emotion behind the message, and instrumental sound has identical power and purpose to communicate in this way.

Individual and collective resonance

As we have seen, resonance influences the mind, body and spirit. It has the power to overcome illness, change human behaviour, shake buildings and demolish cities, but it also plays a fundamental role in our day-to-day lives, often making sense of who we are and the way we behave.

Resonance can also be symbolic of the life force within us. It can influence our direction in life, increase self-awareness, and develop inner peace and harmony through a greater understanding of the way God sees and hears us. Resonance is not just the force which holds all things together, but for those who are able to hear, it can also measure how well all things are working.

"We know that the whole creation has been groaning as in the pains of childbirth right up to the present time. Not only so, but we ourselves, who have the first fruits of the spirit, groan inwardly as we wait eagerly for our adoption, the redemption of our bodies … In the same way, the Spirit helps us in our weakness. We do not know what we ought to pray for, but the Spirit himself intercedes for us through wordless groans." (Romans 8:22–23, 26)

We have established that all matter pulsates with the life of God. Every inanimate object across the universe emits a frequency which is part of that original creation command, and everything which lives and breathes on the earth has its own personal sound. But what of the human being, made in the image of God, yet able to choose whether or not to acknowledge and walk with Him?

Scientific fact dictates that all things vibrate at a specific frequency and the Bible indicates that this is an outworking of the process of Creation through the voice of God. This is a quite separate matter to individuals choosing to acknowledge that voice or recognise they are a part of it. Both fact and process remain unchanged. Therefore, every human life is a unique creation with a unique frequency and resonance both in and before God.

Imagine, therefore, the power released in an individual who comes into alignment or entrainment with the voice and purposes of the Father, acknowledging and resonating with the frequency placed within! But what is the nature of the frequency of a human being? Is it based on body, mind or spirit, on the life being lived or the activities being carried out on a day-to-day basis?

We know that the body is made up of many parts, each a separate unit relating to the purpose and function of the whole. Unlike inanimate objects with a single vibration, each of the body's units vibrates at its own rate, the proof of which can be seen in the use of the ultrasound to shatter kidney and gall stones through the identification of their specific frequency within the body.

Similar principles have been used to shrivel certain types of cancerous tumours with various degrees of success, and a number of medical companies are beginning to research the frequency range of each body organ. The vibration of each part contributes to the body's collection of multiple frequencies or "collective resonance".

It stands to reason, therefore, that the human body in common with other animal species emits a range of frequencies rather than just one. Such frequencies may represent a personal "harmony" or "song" which will almost certainly be developing and changing as each body part becomes more or less prominent depending on activity, condition and maturity.

Research into DNA, the genetic make up of all life forms, provides further evidence of the unique resonance of every living thing. Researchers across the world have been pioneering a process known as **datasonification**[5], converting information stored in numerical form for computer analysis into sound or musical formation. The process has been successful in a number of different areas including the sonification of DNA data.

Although prevented by law from storing or copyrighting any human data converted in this way, the process has been used to "sonify" the DNA of a number of plants, animals and illnesses such as cancer. The process has also been used to sonify the character and movements of natural phenomena such as earthquakes and volcanoes which change the nature of their sound as they become more active, and to compose musical pieces, creating a new genre known as "DNA", "genome" or "protein" music.

Though the DNA of all human beings is around 98% identical, 2% of the genetic strands are unique to each individual. Converting such information to musical notes confirms the unique identity of every human being, a potential song at the core of every single life.

This too is a resonance of the original voice of God, uniquely recognisable to God himself for all eternity. As Cain discovered after murdering Abel, his brother:

"The Lord said, 'What have you done? Listen! Your brother's blood cries out to me from the ground.'" (Genesis 4:10)

There are many ways, therefore, for an individual to resonate, through a unique combination of resonant frequencies and a unique combination of genetic DNA structures, through thoughts, speech and the everyday actions of life. All are made complete when redeemed and aligned with God's purposes. Imagine then, the collective resonance of a family, group of friends, church or community. Imagine the unique frequencies and harmonies created across a village, town or city and how those harmonies change as new people arrive and others depart.

Imagine the resonance of a nation or continent, each distinct with the expressions, patterns and lifestyles representative of each tribe and nation, the nature of its sound changing as it becomes more aligned with God's purposes.

Imagine the impact in the heavenlies on the principalities and powers over geographical areas as the resonance of the nations becomes more entrained with the sound of heaven and the purposes of God.

In "God Vibrations", Dan McCollam proposes the theory that the distinct musical sounds of instruments across nations and geographical areas could be linked to the pulling down of strongholds and principalities of those areas. He believes that the power to take nations and maintain "air superiority" over the spiritual forces present there lies in the authenticity of the sounds produced and released by the Church living and serving in that area. Sounds produced by the instruments and styles of other nations do not have the same level of authority in that region, which may bring new meaning to:

"How can we sing the songs of the Lord while in a foreign land?" (Psalm 137:4)

The earth itself varies in its vibration rate of 6 to 10Hz, but it also emits an a infinite and changing number of frequencies from every individual, community and nation, every plant, animal, rock formation, river, ocean and all of their activity. Yet as the source of each frequency, God hears and recognises every one. Such broad harmony, one gargantuan collective resonance, is typical of the symphony which has pulsated across the universe since the beginning of time.

The call of the musical prophet is to align him or herself with the sound and purposes of God and to be fully reliant on the Holy Spirit, bringing both the intimacy and power of God to an individual, community, city, situation or nation with the resonance of heaven to call out, create, challenge, destroy or bring breakthrough as the Lord wills and directs.

Endnotes

1. Information on String and Superstring theory can be found on "The Official String Theory Web Site": www.superstringtheory.com

2. I am profoundly grateful and indebted to Dan McCollam, member of the teaching staff of Bethel Church's School of Supernatural Worship and Director of Sounds of the Nations and the Institute for Worship Arts Resources for confirming, extending and increasing my own

thoughts, research and knowledge in this area. For further information on Bethel Church and Dan McCollam, visit: www.ibethel.org and www.ibethel.org/staff/bssw

3. Dan McCollam, God Vibrations, A Christian Perspective on the Power of Sound (DVD Teaching Series produced through the Institute for Worship and Arts Resources by Sound Wisdom Media).

4. A vibrating plate or membrane enabling the effects of sound waves to be viewed. The plate was invented by Ernst Chladni (1756–1827) a German physicist and musician, sometimes referred to as the "Father of Acoustics".

5. Many websites carry information on the reality of and research into datasonification. The following represent a fraction of those available:

LHC Sound:
www.lhcsound.hep.ucl.ac.uk/index.html

Listen to the Higgs Boson:
www.news.discovery.com/space/listen-to-the-higgs-boson-120710.htm

Scientific sonification project:
www.mcs.anl.gov/~kaper/Sonification

Sense aware:
www.sense-aware.com/2010/07/human-dna-genetic-data-sonifications.html

The Artist as Scientist:
www.scribd.com/doc/125144930/The-Artist-as-Scientist-The-Sonification-of-DNA

Human genome music:

www.toddbarton.com/content/music/genome.shtml

Symphony of life:

www.guardian.co.uk/music/2010/jun/24/dna-genome-music-
michael-zev-gordon

6. The Musical Prophet

As we have discovered, sound and music are both fundamental to humanity. They define who we are as a race, tribe or individual, enable us to connect with God and with each other, and have the capacity to bring healing or to destroy.

Yet, as powerful as they are, as forms of expression both sound and music do actually need to be expressed in order for their potential to be released. The resonant frequency of a wine glass only sounds if the glass itself is struck. The beauty of a violin melody can only be appreciated if it is actually heard. Likewise, the power of music can only be realised if it is played.

Music is a powerful means through which both Man and God can share their heart and mind, and is one of a number of ancient prophetic expressions being revived in the Church today. As an emotional and spiritual form of communication, music is able to facilitate a transformation of feeling, thought and memory through the power of the Holy Spirit using a host of interdependent sensory capabilities.

The prophetic musician or "musical prophet" is an instigator and enabler of much of this activity, but how is such a role fulfilled? What skills and qualities are essential in the development of the musical prophet and what characterises the man or woman taking on this role?

Two roles

In the light of Scripture, the musical prophet has two key roles:

• To bring the heart and mind of God to a situation, individual or community

• To create prophetic atmospheres in which others may hear God and prophesy for themselves

The first of these is the more traditionally accepted role for any prophet – someone who receives and delivers a word direct from God to an individual or community. But how does this type of "word" develop for the musical prophet?

The development of a word will depend very much on how God speaks to the prophet receiving it, how he or she functions in the realm of the Holy Spirit, its context and the place where it is given.

The term "word" may still be used, as God will be communicating through the music, even though there is little spoken language involved.

A word may come to the prophet as an emotion or a feeling, as a single expression, a sentence or a passage of Scripture. It may be a picture or a sequence of events. It could involve just one emotion or it may develop from one to another. It could be a dream or an understanding of a situation which God wishes to touch. In this respect, the development of the word can be similar to that of spoken prophecy, and sometimes that is how the word may present itself. However, it is the outworking of the musical prophecy which will differ considerably to a spoken word.

To bring the prophetic musically is to bring a sense of the Holy Spirit's leading to the listener through one's playing, through a mood or feeling, a theme, melody or pattern of notes, a chord sequence, a style or a complete piece of music. Beyond a sense of what God is bringing, or recognising an inherent emotion, it is not necessary for the musician to know exactly *how* God is speaking, but he/she can allow the Holy Spirit to bring the detail and precision directly to the listener through the music. This not only releases the musician from trying to understand the detail of the word logically, but also prevents serious repercussions of any false interpretation of the situation. It also releases the listener directly into the intimacy and love of God.

Sometimes the sense of what the Holy Spirit wishes to bring will come immediately and, at other times, it will take some serious thought and effort. Very rarely will a complete musical prophecy come miraculously "from above". More often than not, it will take effort, determination and sacrifice to grow in this ministry – a combination of the skilled musician developing in the prophetic, the worshipper listening to the Holy Spirit and a desire to bring release and growth to the individual or community. As David said,

"I insist on paying the full price. I will not take for the Lord what is yours, or sacrifice a burnt offering that costs me nothing." (1 Chronicles 21:24)

Taking an idea, thought, sentence or just "a sense of" and building it into a prophetic musical piece will demand determination, focus, sacrifice, time and understanding.

Atmosphere creators

The second of these roles, to create atmospheres in which others may hear God and prophesy for themselves, is a relatively new revelation to the Church today, but was a standard practice in Old and New Testament times.

Atmosphere can be defined in a number of ways. It may refer to the gases surrounding the earth, the air pressure which creates weather patterns across geographical areas or the prevailing mood brought about by circumstances and relationships surrounding an individual or group of people. All three realities are governed by the spiritual realm created by the combination of prevailing spiritual forces, the angelic and, as Paul calls them the "principalities", "powers" and the "prince of the power of the air" (Ephesians 6, 12 and 2:2 NKJV). In the same way that music is often the creating force of the atmosphere in a film or social gathering, music created by a musical prophet or team of discerning worshippers directed towards the Creator can bring change in the realms of spiritual atmosphere.

Throughout the Old Testament in particular, musicians were often called upon by prophets to create or change the spiritual atmosphere so that they could hear God. In 2 Kings, for example, Jehoshaphat, king of Judah asks the prophet Elisha for a word from the Lord. Elisha, as awesome a prophet as he was, was unable to bring any word until the atmosphere had been changed by a visiting musician:

"'But now bring me a musician.' Then it happened, when the musician played, that the hand of the Lord came upon him. And he said, 'Thus says the Lord...'"[2] (2 Kings 3:15–16 NKJV)

On many occasions Saul had encounters with prophets. Through his meeting at Gibeah (1 Samuel 10:10) he was "changed into a different person". The change was so intense that Saul began to prophesy himself:

"When all those who had formerly known him saw him prophesying with the prophets, they asked each other, 'What is this that has happened to the son of Kish? Is Saul also among the prophets?'" (1 Samuel 10:11)

The prophetic atmosphere here was such that a man, who earlier in the day had simply been looking for his father's donkeys, runs into God, is totally transformed, meets his destiny and begins to prophesy with the company of prophets.

As king of Israel, Saul gradually descended into rebellion against God, but when brought into his presence by an individual or group of prophets, he was able to find God again. Scripture indicates that David's prophetic musicianship regularly created an atmosphere which brought Saul refreshment and healing. Even at his most rebellious and murderous state, after sending three groups of men to capture David, Saul, just as the men he had sent before him, is deeply transformed by an encounter with God through the prophetic atmosphere which had been created:

"Word came to Saul: 'David is in Naioth at Ramah'; so he sent men to capture him. But when they saw a group of prophets prophesying, with Samuel standing there as their leader, the Spirit of God came on Saul's men, and they also prophesied. Saul was told about it, and he sent more men, and they prophesied too. Saul sent men a third time, and they also prophesied. Finally, he himself left for Ramah and went to the great cistern at Seku. And he asked, 'Where are Samuel and David?' 'Over in Naioth at Ramah,' they said. So Saul went to Naioth at Ramah. But the Spirit of God came even on him, and he walked along prophesying until he came to Naioth. He stripped off his garments, and he too prophesied in Samuel's presence. He lay naked all that day and all that night. This is why people say, 'Is Saul among the prophets?'" (1 Samuel 19:19–24)

In the New Testament, Paul and Silas, beaten, flogged and

thrown into prison changed the spiritual atmosphere through their praying and singing:

"About midnight Paul and Silas were praying and singing hymns to God, and the other prisoners were listening to them. Suddenly there was such a violent earthquake that the foundations of the prison were shaken. At once all the prison doors flew open, everyone's chains came loose. The jailer woke up, and when he saw the prison doors open, he drew his sword and was about to kill himself because he thought the prisoners had escaped. But Paul shouted, 'Don't harm yourself! We are all here!' The jailer called for lights, rushed in and fell trembling before Paul and Silas. He then brought them out and asked, 'Sirs, what must I do to be saved?'" (Acts 16:25–30)

As a result of their praises, Paul and Silas had brought about an atmospheric change. God visited the prison, setting people free both physically and spiritually and no one wanted to leave. As a result, the jailer and his family were saved.

An encounter with God is life changing for anyone, whatever their state of mind, spirit or body, their philosophy, whether believer or non-believer, God-seeker or in rebellion. Psalm 22 states, "You are holy, enthroned in the praises of Israel" (Psalm 22:3 NKJV). As the Body of Christ and the expression of God on earth today he inhabits our praises, manifesting his glory, pouring out his Spirit on all present, bringing freedom, transformation and destiny. His desire is to pour out his Spirit on all flesh, inviting everyone to be involved.

The musical prophet has the authority not just to deliver specific words to individuals or communities, but to create the spiritual atmosphere where the presence of God may be manifest in the very ways we have read about in both Old and New Testaments. In this role, the prophet opens a door to the heavenlies, a gateway or portal where the grace, mercy and love of God become available to all. Psalm 100 is very clear on both principle and process:

"Enter His gates with thanksgiving, and His courts with praise; give thanks to him and praise his name. For the Lord is good and his love endures for ever; his faithfulness continues through all generations." (Psalm 100:4–5)

Is it any wonder then that as we begin to follow biblical principles and practices, we begin to see the demonstrations, signs and wonders we read about?

So how is a spiritual atmosphere created or changed in this way? As we have seen, the Lord creates and changes atmospheres by his presence; we do not. However, the manner in which we worship can help or hinder this process.

Giving thanks, declaring his goodness, proclaiming his greatness, singing his praises, testifying to his love, power and truth will create the very atmosphere that the Lord loves to inhabit. But how does one prepare for this musically?

For the musical prophet, there are many options in creating the specific atmosphere which the Lord wishes to bring to a church, community or city. The choice of sounds, chord types and combinations, melodic lines, musical styles and instrumental timbres will focus the atmosphere into one through which the Lord will speak, direct and presence himself.

The principles are the same whether the atmosphere is being created at a Christian gathering or a secular event, whether it is taking place indoors or out on the street. Though the reception of those present may differ initially, the whole earth is the Lord's and, as believers, we carry the glory of God and the power to change spiritual environments and prepare for the miraculous in exactly the same way as we read about in Scripture.

Though not quite so specific as an individual or community prophecy, the process of creating an atmosphere musically is very similar to that of a prophetic word, in that it relies on the way in which the Holy Spirit speaks to the musical prophet, through a thought, word or sentence, an emotion or feeling, or a picture, dream or sequence of events. The starting point musically for the atmosphere will be specific to the time, location and purpose of the gathering and the musical atmosphere will be the foundation for all other prophetic activity taking place.

Worshipping and prophesying purely through the sound of the instrument is a powerful medium and atmosphere creator in its own right and particularly effective in the context of a street gathering. Other activities or forms of communication are not necessarily needed. As worship is a matter of the whole being, and of spirit and truth, expressing the heart through the musical instrument is a powerful statement in heavenly places. As a spiritual tool, sound creates and changes atmosphere without any need for verbalisation or vocabulary, and as supernatural forces both music and sound can create or destroy. These principles and the musical options available to the musical prophet are presented in the following chapter.

Skills, qualities and character

As a communicator of God's heart and mind, the core skills and qualities characterising those involved in prophetic music will be the same as those of any believer involved in any type of prophetic ministry. Prophetic music must never be seen as different to or more important than any other area of prophetic gift. The form and format may differ, but its purpose is the same and so are the roles and responsibilities. It is also important not to invent a false set of criteria for the prophet to measure up to. Scripture is clear enough on the character and qualities which define leadership and though track record is an important safeguard for the Church, everyone has to start somewhere.

As with anyone serving in the body of Christ, the qualities essential in making a difference to others are all matters of the heart. Relationship with God is key and therefore giving to and receiving from him is central to being who we are and everything we do. David was described by God as "a man after my own heart" (Acts 13:22) and whether we have been believers for a few weeks or for many years, the desire for God and movement towards rather than away from him are far more important than any giftings or skills.

As a prophetic musician, however, it is essential to actually be a musician, as the term implies. Being a musician means many things to many people, from the accomplished classical pianist, the skilled rock guitarist or versatile vocalist, to someone who has started to take lessons on an instrument. David was a skilled musician and this would have transformed the music he played, since the development of skill always improves the quality, breadth and depth of any creative work.

However, at some point in his life, David must have picked up the harp for the first time and his passion for God would have found a new expression. This was probably one of the keys to his pursuit of musical excellence and growth as a prophet. We must not think, therefore, that musicians in the early stages of their belief or musical development will be unable to hear or interpret the voice of God until they have reached maturity, either in their faith or musical skill. This simply isn't scriptural and doesn't bear witness to Church history.

Much of the dynamism of the early Church was brought through God using relatively new converts. In the same way, much of the freshness and newness of expression in worship flooding the Church across the world today is being brought by young believers. Though the depth of what is brought and the way it is brought musically may be embryonic, it is the passion for God which overflows no matter what the skill level or faith experience. In the same way that Paul says, "Eagerly desire spiritual gifts, especially the gift of prophecy" and "I would like every one of you to speak in tongues, but even more to prophesy" (1 Corinthians 14) so every believer who plays a musical instrument has the potential to bring the prophetic musically.

It is important here to distinguish between instrumental and vocal prophecy. In this study, we are not examining the role of the vocalist, who may be inspired by the Holy Spirit to bring a prophetic song. The use of any recognisable sentence structure, even though musical, would define such expression as an extension of spoken prophecy – though use of some words creatively may actually enhance the processes we are investigating. We are instead focussing here on the role and nature of instrumental music and the instrumentalist.

The musical prophet, in common with all prophetic believers, is primarily a listener – someone who senses the Holy Spirit's lead and then brings the heart and mind of God to a situation, individual or community through musical rather than oral expression.

Bob Sorge writes,

"By playing with sensitivity to the Spirit, a musician can do more in a few minutes to cause people's hearts to open to the Lord than three hours of preaching ever could."[1]

In the same way that praying in tongues can bypass the brain's understanding of a situation and can therefore be more effective spiritually, the musical interpretation of a word may bypass the mind allowing God to speak directly to the heart. Such is the power of the musician when skill is matched with an ear open to the Holy Spirit.

In the passage from Joshua 6 referred to earlier, it is interesting that the priests carried their instruments around Jericho for six days and then another seven times on the seventh day, before actually playing them. This may have been purely symbolic, a reverse of Sabbath law, but it could have suggested a perfect time proportion set aside to listen to God and wait for his anointing and power to come before taking action.[2]

Musicians can often find difficulty in silence or laying down their instrument, yet the preparation time for developing a word, particularly when there is a complex situation to be addressed, will almost always be longer than the word itself. Musicians are also renowned for hiding behind their instruments and technical ability. Though the priests were physically marching behind the instruments they were carrying in this passage, it would appear this was a symbolic act, presenting their instruments and abilities to God to take as his own and use for his purposes. The result was astonishing!

Musical prophets are warriors, experts in fighting the enemy, often found on the front line or involved in guerrilla warfare tactics. All three Old Testament passages referred to earlier in this study involved warfare on some level. David was "a brave man and a warrior"(1 Samuel 16:18); the musicians leading the prophets down from the high place in 1 Samuel 10 were entering a town with a dangerous enemy garrison; and the act of the Israelites against Jericho was one of the key military strategies of the Old Testament.

We know that worship leaders often face enemy attack, as they are involved in leading God's people into truth and taking back enemy territory. The same can be said for the musical prophet, whose role involves hearing God's strategies, engaging tactically in defence from and attack of the enemy, rescuing individuals or communities from past injuries and current problems, and often engaging in enemy territory through musical prophecy.

Musical prophets are first and foremost worshippers of God and secondly servants in the body of Christ. They understand the significance of the commandments Jesus called the greatest:

"Hearing that Jesus had silenced the Sadducees, the Pharisees got together. One of them, an expert in the law, tested him with this question: 'Teacher, which is the greatest commandment in the law?' Jesus replied: '"Love the Lord your God with all your heart and with all your soul and with all your mind." This is the first and greatest commandment. And the second is like it: "Love your neighbour as yourself." All the Law and the Prophets hang on these two commandments.'" (Matthew 22:34–40)

Far more central to his life than skilled musician, warrior or king, David was a worshipper and a lover of God. He knew the truth of who God is, the purpose of life and his position in it. For most of his time as a king he would have experienced a lavish lifestyle with fame and fortune, yet he remained a humble and honest worshipper to the end of his days, a servant king after God's heart.

Many musicians today can experience a similar lavish lifestyle with equivalent doses of fame and fortune, and sometimes overnight success where life's reality can become distorted.

Christian musicians are not exempt from this. It can be all too easy to lose sight of the Giver as the gift grows, to allow one's love for God and neighbours to grow cold and one's passion for worship and service to be replaced by the message or the music presented. In his teaching on spiritual gifts, Paul states,

"If I speak in human or angelic tongues, but do not have love, I am only a resounding gong or a clanging cymbal. If I have the gift of prophecy and can fathom all mysteries and all knowledge, and if I have faith that can move mountains, but do not have love, I am nothing." (1 Corinthians 13:1–2)

Humility and love are keys to understanding how and why the prophetic works as it does. The desire to grow in prophecy of any type has to be rooted in love, to bring release to the captive, often from agony into destiny, and to love one's brother and sister enough to eagerly desire what is best for them, to prophesy orally or musically from a desire to see them blessed, set free and liberated into their calling, rather than glorifying oneself in a gift which has been freely given to us. The harp was an extension of David's life in God. It was never a throne or a block to it.

Endnotes

1. Bob Sorge, Exploring Worship, (Oasis House, 1987)
2. The "musician" or "zamar" (Hebrew) in this passage is often translated as "harpist" or "minstrel", suggesting a prophetic wanderer and atmosphere changer.

7. Musical Choices

If musical prophecy is something in which you are becoming interested or you feel a passion developing for prophetic music, where do you start? How does a musical prophet begin to create music with a prophetic edge or compose a musical prophecy? What are the basics and how do you develop skill in this area?

Creating a musical prophecy is no different practically to composing any other piece of music. Understanding what music is and what it can do is a great start. Becoming familiar with the essential components that make music what it is and understanding how they can be manipulated or developed into an expression of the heart is the next major step to take. In the area of musical prophecy, understanding and skill develop hand in hand.

Decisions

All music is the result of a series of choices, personal experience and purpose set within a time frame and location. Each musical piece is the product of who we are, where we are and when we are. It is also shaped by what we are creating and why we are creating it.

As musical prophets, how and what we create is very much the result of our character, the knowledge and experience we have absorbed both musically and spiritually and the instruments we play. There is no one type, pattern or standard of prophetic music, but the musical decisions and choices we make will be greatly influenced by where we are and the times in which we live.

Johann Sebastian Bach, for example, didn't compose for the saxophone because it had not yet been invented. Beethoven was unlikely to use the harpsichord in his composition work as it had been overshadowed by the pianoforte. Similarly, 21st Century musicians of the Middle East are unlikely to use the jazz styles of London or New York and creators of Western contemporary dance music are unlikely to use formal dance styles popular in the Tudor period. We are all products of our own contemporary culture. As musical prophets, therefore, we need to bear this in mind when creating to ensure we remain relevant to the society in which we live.

The basics

In practical terms music is, in essence, a combination of created elements – pitch, duration, rhythm, speed, dynamics, instrumentation, timbre, texture and structure. The manner in which elements are combined or the emphasis placed on each individual element will affect the character and direction of any piece of music or musical prophecy.

A working understanding of these elements is useful for all musicians when first developing their gifting and is essential in growing in both spiritual and musical wisdom.

Musical elements are often best understood in primary and secondary terms. Primary elements are those essential to create (or even play) a basic piece of music. Secondary elements are important in making decisions about detail or the finer points of the piece and to develop the knowledge and technique necessary to combine sounds, instruments and styles of music. Secondary musical elements add infinite levels of variety and interest to any musical creation.

Primary Elements

Harmony – a combination of chords providing a framework around which other musical elements such as melody are often centred.

An understanding of harmony is vital to every musician, even if the instrument you play is not a harmony instrument or the type of music performed has no audible harmony part. In the same way that rhythm often defines the style of a musical piece, harmony usually helps define its character and sound.

Harmony not only characterises the flavour of supporting

instruments and voices, but of a whole band, orchestra or choir, as the notes of both instrumental and vocal parts will be derived from the harmony of the piece. Even the notes of a solo melody line will be based on the understanding of some form of harmony, whether or not any underlying harmony part exists.

Knowledge of harmony will not just enable you to increase the number of chords you are able to master, but will expand the whole of your musical vocabulary, opening up huge potential to express more fully the heart of God.

Melody – a connected pattern of notes/pitches.

Melody is often the most prominent feature of a musical work and frequently committed to memory by the listener long before harmony or any other element is recognised. For many listeners, melody actually defines a piece of music and is often the principal reason behind its triumphant success or dismal failure.

At its simplest, melody is a series of notes linked together to form a continuous musical line, but a successful melody is much more than that. It is a unique expression of the composer and a combination of many different factors.

As such the melody of any piece cannot be developed in isolation but is dependant upon most other musical elements.

Rhythm – the duration of individual notes and silences within a musical part.

Rhythm is a part of everyday life, affecting much of what we do, incorporating beat and repetition as well as episodes of unpredictability. Rhythm exists at the very core of every musical expression and affects every creative aspect and thought.

Secondary Elements

Speed/Tempo – the pace at which a piece is played.

Volume/Dynamics – how loud or soft a piece, or section of a piece, is or becomes.

Instrumentation – the choice of individual or combinations of instruments.

Timbre – the character or feel of an individual instrument or voice.

Texture – the character or feel of a combination of instruments or voices.

Structure and style

Another essential layer of the creative process is the structure of the musical piece from beginning to end, and the musical style in which it is conceived. Both structure and style make sense of the work, setting it within a context of both time and place.

These three elemental areas of music represent the basics or building blocks of any piece of music. A working understanding of them not only improves the quality of sounds and pieces produced, but also serves as a thorough grounding both musically and spiritually when putting the prophetic into practice, preventing stagnation and increasing the knowledge of musical vocabulary through which the Lord can share his heart, thoughts and personality more fully.

John's gospel says:

"To the Jews who had believed him, Jesus said 'If you hold to my teaching, you are really my disciples. Then you will know the truth and the truth will set you free.'" (John 8:32)

The implication of this statement is that it is the truth you know which will set you free, not just the truth that has always existed as reality. Consequently, it is the revelation and knowledge of the ways of the Holy Spirit which is empowering so many to reconnect with God in these days, not the ways themselves, which have always existed.

In the same way, it is the knowledge of how music communicates both emotionally and spiritually, as well as coming to terms with the nuts and bolts, the theory and practice of music, which will empower the musician to encompass more of the breadth, depth, length and height of the personality and love of God in any creative work. David was a skilled musician as well as a worshipper and warrior. Becoming a skilled musician, as opposed to just a musician requires understanding and practical training, meditation and practice, opportunity and feedback. It won't just happen without actually engaging in the process. It is learning how to interpret a situation, need or "word", developing a listening ear and the ability to discern what the Holy Spirit brings in all humility which will bring release and breakthrough to the lives of individuals and communities as well as your own.

"Trust in the Lord with all your heart and lean not on your own understanding; in all your ways submit to him, and he will make your paths straight. Do not be wise in your own eyes; fear the Lord and shun evil. This will bring health to your body and nourishment to your bones." (Proverbs 3:5–8)

8. What, Where, Who, How And When?

After reading this brief introduction, there is a good chance that you will have been persuaded of the power of both music and sound, and the need for prophetic music and/or musical prophecy today. There is an even greater chance, however, that the Holy Spirit will have been confirming this already and an excitement, passion or even a perceivable calling is beginning to rise within you. How do you make the first move, find out more about the role and begin to take on assignments?

What, where and how?

There is tremendous scope and possibility in the role and remit of the musical prophet. However, there are often just two distinct types of assignment.

Firstly, the musical prophet may be empowered to change

the spiritual atmosphere of a specific location. This could be a building, a specific establishment or organisation, a street, town, city or nation, bringing the sound and authority of heaven to that place.

In this context, the musical prophet has the authority to work wherever the Lord leads within the framework of the law and humility. Permission may sometimes be needed to "play music" within the confines of an organisation, establishment or building and a licence will often be required to "perform" in the streets of a town or city. However, just as any other "busker", details of the style and purpose of the music are not required and would be rarely understood by those giving permission or issuing a licence.

Secondly, the musical prophet may be authorised to bring the voice of God to a specific situation, individual or community.

In this type of assignment, when prophesying into the life or situation of an individual or church community, permission or an invitation to do so needs to be given by the individual or the person who has responsibility/authority within the church. Though words are rarely spoken in prophetic music, the musical prophet can yield tremendous influence. Therefore a leader or someone with oversight for the individual or community must cover any ministry taking place. When prophesying into the life of a town, city or nation, some form of permission should be sought where available and appropriate.

However, generally, in a secular setting, there will be little understanding of this ministry or concept and so with a humble heart and sincere desire to serve the community, authority may be received direct from the Father.

Depending on the type of assignment, the musical prophet may work alone or as part of an ensemble or band of like-minded members, and even as part of an orchestra as the scale of this type of ministry grows. Musical prophecy is equally effective in both sacred and secular settings (in God, all settings are as one) and amongst both believing and non-believing groups. It is important to recognise that for the prophet, the Holy Spirit, not the setting or the group, is the source of all power, authority and inspiration, whatever the situation, setting or circumstance.

Working in a solo capacity is usually straightforward, though the pace at which you develop as a musical prophet and the quality of the "words" you bring will depend largely upon the time and effort you are able to put into training on your instrument, development in spiritual awareness and your devotion to God. Through taking instrumental lessons, following a recognised programme of study or devising your own you will develop significant musical expertise and develop an understanding of how working links into the realm of the Holy Spirit are made. Through developing your relationship with God as an active worshipper, becoming a listener first and a communicator or doer second, you will develop a passion, devotion and authority just as David did.

In establishing an ensemble or band, a greater degree of understanding between the team members will need to be developed, not just in hearing God together for a situation, individual or community, but in the practicalities, communication and direction of harmony, structure, style etc. As atmosphere changers working in new styles and patterns, without the security of a Sunday morning set list or any familiar method of "leading worship", close ties between the team members will need to be made both musically and spiritually. This is not really an area that can be standardised, but one that needs to be pioneered. Every team will be different in its personalities, giftings and ways of working.

Occasionally there will be time to plan for an event or a specific prophetic word, but more often there will not. Sometimes, the issue or situation needing a "word" will be known to you in advance, but more often it will not. At times the meaning of the "word" being played will remain a mystery to the prophet, but will bring tremendous communication between the individual or community and God. This is absolutely fine. As listeners first, we will become used to working in all sorts of situations and settings, and often will not need to know the issues.

It is also essential to have some form of support from or accountability to others, either from a local church or expression of the Kingdom with which you are involved or from an emerging network or group. This is for your own protection and blessing in a spiritually volatile world as well as honouring those to whom you are ministering.

Who and when?

We all carry the glory of God and as Jesus' friends and disciples we walk under the open heaven which he himself brought (Matthew 3:16). In all we are and all we do in our lives we can choose to worship Jesus. With all we have, both seen and unseen, we are witnesses to the principalities, powers and nations of the world that Jesus is Lord. Our interests and giftings, our home and work lives are there as offerings, available for him to use. Whether we consider ourselves beginners or experts in any type of skill, we all have ears and hearts available for God to use for his glory.

Prophecy is the revealing of God's voice, ways and purpose to those whom we meet on a day-to-day basis, should they choose to listen. As walking testimonies of God's grace, mercy and transforming power, we are all prophets. Where music plays an active interest or part in our lives through the pursuit of an instrumental skill, we have the capacity to be musical prophets. As Paul writes,

"I would like every one of you to speak in tongues, but even more to prophesy." (1 Corinthians 14:5)

With an ear to hear and a determination of heart to pursue excellence and skill as David did, we are all able to bring the voice of God though what we play. Of course, there will always be those with greater levels of skill and understanding to bring a deeper revelation of God's ways or a more accomplished musical interpretation, but that does not prevent anyone from bringing their talent to God in this way. Anyone can bring the sound of heaven to the street no matter how short a time they have been playing. Anyone who is listening can bring a level of comfort and peace to someone, for it is the heart before God and the involvement of the Holy Spirit which counts. Musical prophecy is for everyone who wishes to pursue it.

There are those who will say there is no difference between musical prophecy and improvisatory styles such as jazz, or programmes such as music or sound therapy. However, in the same way that today's worship songs are separate in purpose from secular songs, even though their musical styles are often similar, it is the direction in which prophecy is focussed, the spirit with which it is presented and the involvement of the Holy Spirit himself which keeps musical prophecy holy.

The question of "when?" is a very interesting one in relation to the reestablishment of prophetic music in the Kingdom. Nationally there has never been such interest in the scientific properties of sound. From healing to gaining a better understanding of the universe, there have been countless research articles, magazine and newspaper reports and recent television documentaries about the power and properties of sound.

Spiritually, the Church as a whole is taking steps towards embracing the supernatural nature of its calling and beginning to see signs of the miraculous on a daily basis. There is also much talk in a number of influential circles about the "sound of heaven" and the spiritual significance of the sound of specific instruments. In the UK during 2012, the nation welcomed the world to the Olympic Games with a national ringing of bells and Queen Elizabeth's Diamond Jubilee River pageant was preceded by a barge of ringing "church" bells. Events around the world such as these continue to have spiritual significance across the nations.

From the creation of the universe by the voice of God to the angels' announcement of Jesus' birth, sound has always been used to both create and proclaim the new. Every move of God has pioneered new sounds and expressions. Every lasting change in society has been accompanied by new musical styles and attitudes. As the Church regains its spiritual heritage and authority and as both society and the Kingdom begin to discover the full potential of music and sound, it would appear that some of the greatest spiritual and social opportunities in history are almost upon us.

9. This Is For Everyone

If you are excited at everything you have read and feel a passion rising to see God work in this way, then it's probably time to investigate this whole area further.

There has never been an easier time to develop and run with God in your calling, or support those around you in theirs. Jesus is on the move like never before in history, restoring his Kingdom's values, principles, gifts and weapons. The Holy Spirit is beginning to challenge our man-made boundaries, whether they are sacred or secular, in the Church or the world, believer or non-believer. God is pouring out his Spirit on all flesh just as he promised He would. The veil between heaven and earth is thinning. Heaven itself is breaking out onto the streets, into the bars and nightclubs, shops, schools, governments and the local church and prophetic music is playing a fundamental role in the process. The musical prophet is a key worker in the restoration of heaven on earth, bringing God's heart and voice to sacred and secular, Church and world, believer and non-believer, in a variety of ways, settings and situations.

In my own experience I have seen both individuals and groups of believers released from long-standing illnesses, tormenting mental conditions and demonic oppression through musical prophecy. I have witnessed areas of cities being changed, literally becoming physically and spiritually lighter during periods of declaration in the musically prophetic, and even patterns of public behaviour transformed over longer periods of sustained commitment. In a number of local churches I have observed the release of exuberant worship and seen displays of the fullness of the Holy Spirit through such divine encounters, many in communities where such demonstrations had never been seen or allowed before. I have also seen those who profess no faith at all literally bump into God on the street, discovering their destiny in the same way as Saul did thousands of years ago.

Just go for it

The whole ministry area of the musical prophet is a heart response to God. Whether you are a beginner or seasoned musician, or a new or mature Christian is not important. Spiritual atmospheres may be changed through the obedience and skill of anyone with a heart for him. God can speak and act through you right now. And even if you don't consider yourself a musician, or your call is more focused on pastoring, teaching, intercession or any other ministry, you can be a supporter, encourager, releaser, overseer or "cheerer on" of musical prophecy and the musical prophet.

Just as the prophetic is a significant part of the whole body of Christ, rather than an isolated unit within it, so prophetic music is a significant part of the prophetic not just an isolated unit. Both need nurturing, support, training and oversight within and for the sake of the whole body of Christ.

So, are you raring to go? Do you want to give it a try?

There are a number of things you start doing right now:

1. Choose a quiet place and begin to worship God. Use an instrument and/or voice, but don't use words, and try not to base what you play on the chords or melody line of any other song or piece you know. Wherever possible, invent your own chord sequence, melody or rhythmic pattern, but if this is too difficult to begin with, use one you know, then gradually begin to change and move away from it.

As you begin to worship in this way you will find the sequence, melody or rhythm you are playing begins to create a feeling or atmosphere, which becomes more focused as you play more deeply from the heart of God. You will become aware of musical modifications or developments which you could make to move it on both musically and spiritually.

You may sense the atmosphere of the room change as the Holy Spirit becomes more fully present. You may sense God speak into your life or that of your community, and as the music develops he will reveal more of his heart for you and/or for those around you.

2. Get together with a few like-minded musicians or friends.
Begin to worship as outlined above. In this context where there
is more than one musician, someone will need to actually start
the musical process, taking an initial lead, allowing others to
hear what is played and join in. Then allow others to take a lead
as appropriate. Once again you will find the atmosphere changes
and a revelation of God's heart will follow, this time through the
individuality of each group member, but usually with a shared
understanding of what the Holy Spirit is bringing. The pattern for
the way in which this type of group experience works will reflect
those within the group and the relationship and understanding
shared between them.

3. Train both as musicians and prophets. In order to grow in this
whole area, especially where other individuals or communities
are on the receiving end of such ministry, it will be necessary to
train as both musicians and prophets, to improve the breadth
of musical quality and develop maturity in the life of the Spirit.

There are hundreds of tutorials which will help you to improve
your musical technique and thousands of books and programmes
to develop your prophetic understanding and insight. In
addition, instrumental teachers, prophets and mentors are
incredibly valuable and will always help you on your way. A
series of practical teaching manuals designed to follow on from
this study will also be available from August 2014, delivering
both musical and spiritual training from basic to an advanced
standard, helping you grow in your gift whilst increasing your
passion. Each manual contains exercises in developing creative
ideas within the core studies of harmony, melody and rhythm,

linking each of them to an understanding of their relevance in the Spirit. Further details will be available online from August 2014 through a web search of "The Return of the Musical Prophet".

Is my response important?

As with every gift, calling, skill, ministry or lifestyle there is a choice. Being a pioneer is not easy. You will be misunderstood and open to front line attack because of the power God has invested in you against the enemy. However, responding in obedience to God's call, and seeing his will played out in the lives of individuals and communities through release, healing, atmospheric change and in a host of other ways is a real privilege. And as with any calling, choosing to take on the role of musical prophet not only blesses God and those around you, but will also bless you beyond measure.

So why not give it a go? The life of pioneering and service is always an exciting one. Responding to an inner call will always produce fruit that will last, resulting in salvation and healing. The call and saving grace of God through the role of the musical prophet as a communicator is a precious call bringing liberation to the captive and healing to the sick of heart. It will bring further refinement and wholeness to the body of Christ and will change the course of history for individuals, communities and the nations.

Suggested Reading

Byrd, Andy and Feucht, Sean: *Fire and Fragrance* (Destiny Image, 2010)

De Silva, Dawn: *Shifting atmospheres* (Bethel)

Goodall, Howard, *The Story of Music* (Chatto & Windus)

Haslam, Greg, *Preach the Word*, (Sovereign World, 2006)

Hughes, Ray: *Minstrel Series part 1 and 2 (Selah)* – CD

Hughes, Ray: *The Tabernacle of David. Then and now (Selah)* – CD

Kissell, Barry, *The Prophet's Notebook* (Kingsway Publications, 2002)

McCollam, Dan, *God Vibrations: A Christian perspective on the power of sound* (DVD Teaching Series produced through the Institute for Worship and Arts Resources by Sound Wisdom Media).

McCollam, Dan, *God Vibrations: study guide* (Bethel)

McCollam, Dan and Vallotton, Kris: *Bethel School of Prophets* (Bethel, 2010) – CD / DVD

Powell, John, *How Music Works* (Penguin)

Richer, Margaret, *Understand Music Theory* (Teach Yourself)

Sorge, Bob, *Exploring Worship* (Oasis House, 1987)

About The Author

Steve Abley is the Director of "Burn 24-7" Winchester and a Manager of "Changing Tunes", a charity providing rehabilitation through music to prisoners and ex-prisoners. He is married with a daughter and a member of the Winchester Vineyard Church.

Steve has been involved with music as a composer, performer, teacher and worship leader for most of his adult life. He holds both Bachelor and Master's degrees in Music majoring in classical composition and a Post Graduate Certificate in Education. He taught Music in a variety of schools for over 20 years and still teaches a number of piano students.

Steve's passion lies in leading worshippers of any age, denomination, experience or social group into the manifest presence of God, and in training musicians to take the prophetic sound of heaven onto the streets of the UK and beyond.